Defining the Digital Economy

The Structure of the Digital Economy in Focus

The way things are today does not preclude evolution to a different truth tomorrow.

Defining the Digital Economy

The Structure of the Digital Economy in Focus

Lori Jo Underhill

LJU PRESS

Scottsdale

Defining the Digital Economy by Lori Jo Underhill published by LJU Press
Post Office Box 12452 Scottsdale, Arizona 85267
www.ljuassociates.com
© 2019 Lori Jo Underhill
DASH – Digital Asset Sector Hierarchy © 2018
CoinSector © 2018
All rights reserved.
No portion of this book may be reproduced in any form without permission from the publisher, except as permitted by U.S. copyright law. For permissions contact DefiningtheDigitalEconomy@gmail.com
ISBN: 9781796855159

DEDICATION

To: Rachel Jessi, Sukey, and Josh.

Keeping me accountable. Reminding me who I am.

Contents

CHAPTER 1   1
  EVOLUTION   *1*
    THE WORLD WAS FLAT AND THEN IT WAS NOT   1

CHAPTER 2   4
  DAWN OF THE NEW AGE OF FINANCE   *4*
    THE NEW AGE OF FINANCE   4

CHAPTER 3   7
  JOURNEY   *7*
    THE DIGITAL ECONOMY AND JOURNEY TO BECOME AN INDEPENDENT DIGITAL ECONOMIST   7

CHAPTER 4   10
  STORES OF VALUE, AGREEMENTS, AND CONSENSUS   *10*
    INHERENT STORES OF VALUE ARE BASED ON AGREEMENTS AND OPERATE ON CONSENSUS   10
    STORE OF VALUE   10

CHAPTER 5   13
  ASSETS, DIGITAL ASSETS, AND DIGITAL UNITS   *13*
    ASSET   13
    DIGITAL ASSET   14
    DIGITAL UNIT   15
    MONEY   18
    MONEY VERSUS TRANSACTIONS OR PAYMENTS   18

CHAPTER 6   20
  ECONOMIES   *20*
    ECONOMIES ARE AGREEMENTS THAT OPERATE ON CONSENSUS   20
    ECONOMY   20
    ECONOMIES ARE AGREEMENTS   21
    ECONOMIES OPERATE ON CONSENSUS   22
    INCUMBENT ECONOMY VERSUS DIGITAL ECONOMY   24
    ECONOMIES VERSUS MARKETS   26

CHAPTER 7   27
  INCUMBENT ASSETS VERSUS DIGITAL ASSETS   *27*
    Digital Asset and Digital Unit Fundamentals   27
    Digital Asset Construct Analysis   30
    STORES OF VALUE AND FINANCIAL INSTRUMENTS   33
    COMMODITIES   33
    DIGITAL COMMODITY   34
    CURRENCIES   35

INCUMBENT CURRENCIES	35
DIGITAL CURRENCIES	37
DIGITAL CURRENCY	39
DIGITAL CERTIFICATE OF VALUE	42
DIGITAL EQUITY - INSTRUMENTS OF EXCHANGE OR OWNERSHIP	43
DIGITAL EQUITIES ARE DISTINCT FROM INCUMBENT STOCK EQUITY INSTRUMENTS	44
Manifested Asset	46
Representative Asset	46
Underlying Asset	46

CHAPTER 8 — 50

THE NEW DIGITAL ECONOMY SUMMARIZED — *50*

THE STRUCTURE OF THE DIGITAL ECONOMY	51
Digital Commodity	51
Digital Currency	52
Digital Certificate of Value	52
Digital Equity	53
Digital Unit	53

CHAPTER 9 — 55

THE NEW AGE OF MONEY — *55*

ACKNOWLEGEMENTS

Thanks to the CoinMafia,
Rachel, Josh, John, Tyler, and Andrey.

To the #WarriorPrincesses, you know who you are.

For love and friendship, kind patience, support, honesty, challenges, suggestions, feedback, edits, answering when I call, relentless questions, midnight text messages, emails, and nudges.

For being there.

Without all of you this work would not be possible.

CHAPTER 1

EVOLUTION

THE WORLD WAS FLAT AND THEN IT WAS NOT

At one point in human history the collective group-think was the world was flat. Over time, that assumption was challenged and subsequently evolved; first through hypothetical assertion in 600 BC, then through theoretical scientific proofs, and finally through photos taken from space offering further concrete evidence[1] creating a new assumption that the world is spherical. One day the collective group-think was the world was flat; and then, it was not.

> *The way things are today does not preclude evolution to a different truth tomorrow.*

"Crypto-currency", "tokens", and "coins" are terms used to describe Digital Assets[2] operating in the Digital Economy[3]. These terms are not well defined, and the

---

[1] Some conspiracy theorists still question that the earth is spherical and question the validity of photos taken from space. See https://en.wikipedia.org/wiki/Moon_landing_conspiracy_theories (accessed October 12, 2018)

[2] "Digital Asset" Defined here: An "Asset" is something of value; and can be, but not necessarily, a Store of Value. A Digital Asset is something of value where its form is manifested through computer technology. Digital Asset a more accurate description of these assets than "Crypto-Currency". There are four classes of Digital Assets. Digital Commodities, Digital Currencies, Digital Certificates of Value, Digital Equities. Only one of the four is a "Digital Currency."

[3] Defined here: The "Digital Economy" is an ecosystem of production, consumption, trade transcending

scope of these instruments are both technological and transactional. Digital Assets are challenging the nature of what the world generally understands about the definition of an economy, financial assets, financial instruments, and transactioning in the world's economy.

A significant finding from the study of over 2500 Digital Assets uncovered that Digital Assets are not a single asset class. These assets and digital items fall into four Digital Asset classes and one non-financial identifier; offering the world an opportunity to understand contextualize, frame, communicate, and regulate effectively.

Digital Asset adoption has already started. Stakeholders are seeking clarity, context, and a framework of understanding to operate compliantly.

A failure to rapidly reach a consensus of understanding, definition, and context from stakeholders in world finance will slow the pace to solve many challenges and realize the benefits of Digital Asset integration into the world economy.

Adoption of Digital Assets through organic integration in frictionless ecosystems in the undeveloped and underdeveloped parts of the world are the greatest threat to existing financial instruments, constructs, and infrastructures in the developed world.

Transparency, truth, objectivity, education, agreement, and consensus is required. Collaboration between individuals, communities, entities, institutions, and governments about the definition, function, and nature of these assets will provide understanding,

---

geo-political boundaries where "Digital Assets" operate in a virtual or digital environment as Stores of Value, utility, function where there is agreement and consensus about the value of the Digital Assets exchanged in the ecosystem and the method of transfer between them.

compliance, and a framework of context. This will promote integration of these technologies and instruments into the world's existing financial infrastructure.

Digital Assets are a blend of technology and finance. The technological innovation can be difficult to grasp. This work offers a coherent framework for understanding the structure of the Digital Economy, and defines the instruments operating within it. Consensus is necessary and will contribute to a more seamless ushering in of The New Age of Finance.

CHAPTER 2

DAWN OF THE NEW AGE OF FINANCE

THE NEW AGE OF FINANCE

We have entered the dawn of a New Age of Finance. The Digital Economy contains four new asset classes requiring consensus in definition and understanding. Distinct from the four asset classes is a Digital Unit[4] component that operates on a digital ledger. These components also require understanding and definition.

Opinion: The psychology around the adoption of these new technologies is embroiled in the challenges caused by a fear response to a lack of understanding, knowledge, context, clarity, a threat to vested interests in the status quo, and a loss of control. This results in the uncertainty and the noise of misinformation, disintegration, and misapplication, resulting in FUD - Fear, Uncertainty, and Doubt.[5] The FUD and

---

[4] "Digital Unit" Defined in this writing as: A piece of software that is functional and useful, is not an asset, has no inherent financial value, external financial value, and does not represent an asset or a store of value that has financial value. It could be fungible or non-fungible depending on its use case. The supply of the software could be finite or infinite depending on its use case. The software can be a manifestation of something, or represent something underlying that may, or may not, have utilitarian or economic value; however, the unit itself has no economic value. Examples: A Vote, Identity, Digital Container, Measurement, Store of Information, or Store of Data.

[5] "FUD" Fear, Uncertainty, Doubt often invoked in Digital Economy "Crypto-currency" circles to explain the concern people have around these new technologies or their confidence in them.

mis-information are dominating the narrative and are amplified by media algorithms[6] that promote inciteful dialogue.

It is time to calm the storm. It is time for agreement and consensus about the definition of the Digital Assets now operating in the Digital Economy. It is important. According to the World Bank:

> "While there has been progress toward financial inclusion, an estimated 2 billion adults worldwide don't have a basic account. Globally, 59% of adults without an account cite a lack of enough money as a key reason, which implies that financial services aren't yet affordable or designed to fit low income users. Other barriers to account-opening include distance from a financial service provider, lack of necessary documentation papers, lack of trust in financial service providers, and religion."[7]

Developing nations around the world are rapidly adopting Digital Asset technologies. The lack of infrastructure and services within developing nations cause constituents to have no vested interest in the status quo, because the status quo offers them nothing of value. Constituents remain unbanked with no access to financial services. Their ecosystems are ripe for innovation, and the technologies are quickly adopted in these frictionless environments.

Opinion: Friction in the developed world through psychological pushback, group-think, and influence peddlers working to protect vested interests in the existing infrastructure, will thwart progress and cause innovators to flee. Innovation will be driven to execute in open and welcoming ecosystems. Developed nation-state infrastructures; parties and stakeholders benefitting from and vested in existing systems,

---

[6] "Algorithm" A step-by-step procedure for solving a problem or accomplishing some end https://www.merriam-webster.com/dictionary/algorithm/ (accessed October 2, 2018)
[7] http://www.worldbank.org/en/topic/financialinclusion/brief/achieving-universal-financial-access-by-2020 (Accessed September 21, 2018)

ecosystems, and infrastructure; and uncertain and/or unsupportive regulatory environments will discourage innovation in developed nation-states, causing innovators to migrate toward supportive ecosystems. This will create a paradigm shift in transforming the undeveloped and underdeveloped world into the developed world of the future, causing developed nation-states to lag in innovation progress. The solution is to educate, define, and offer proper regulatory guidance. It is time for a consensus of definition.

CHAPTER 3

JOURNEY

THE DIGITAL ECONOMY AND JOURNEY TO BECOME AN INDEPENDENT DIGITAL ECONOMIST

An objective view of finance and economics was necessary to arrive at the insights revealed by this research. The research was independent and self-funded. No pre-conceived lens or special interest guided the research, observation, view, considerations, or development of the concepts resulting in this work. The idea, concepts, and findings offered are not shrouded in any vested interest other than the author's curiosity. At the time of this writing, the author has never purchased or owned any Digital Assets.

These conditions offered an opportunity for an unbiased high-level analytical view, resulting in an objective deep-dive into the Digital Economy without prejudice.

The journey to produce this work began in November 2017 when a friend asked for help to understand and catalog the fundamentals behind Digital Assets operating in the worldwide Digital Asset exchange traded marketplace. The information did not exist. Fundamentals such as foundational and elemental characteristics, classification, definition, core function, value proposition, and economic sector categorization were not available.

A law education provided experience in analyzing parallels and distinctions. The only way to parse through the process was to frame elements against something already existing and understood, then progressing to a subsequent deeper analysis dissecting parallels and distinctions.

Digital Assets operating in the Digital Economy can be explained by framing them against instruments operating in the Incumbent Economy[8].

The first step was to identify and analyze the foundational nature of each Digital Asset, further progressing into a second level analysis to gain understanding and insights. The work analyzed the vision, intent, and purpose of each project associated with the Digital Asset study subjects.

This process provided the necessary clarity to accomplish this task and create the first repeatable and consistently reproducible fundamental Digital Asset construct: The Digital Asset Sector Hierarchy "DASH". The DASH taxonomy is summarily outlined in the Methodologies Whitepaper[9], the original writing where the framework was first introduced in January of 2018.

The DASH is the result of analysis of over 2500 exchange traded Digital Assets worldwide, the GICS™[10] equivalent for the Digital Economy. The construct offers a

---

[8] "Incumbent Economy" The economy operating without Digital Assets in distinct Digital Asset classes.
[9] "DASH" Methodologies - Digital Asset Sector Hierarchy Whitepaper
https://www.coinsector.io/whitepaper/ (accessed September 1, 2018)
[10] "GICS" https://en.wikipedia.org/wiki/Global_Industry_Classification_Standard (accessed

clear categorization and classification hierarchy applicable to every Digital Asset across the spectrum, to identify a Digital Asset's asset class, and determine the economic sector where the Digital Asset operates.

September 22, 2018)

CHAPTER 4

STORES OF VALUE, AGREEMENTS, AND CONSENSUS

INHERENT STORES OF VALUE ARE BASED ON AGREEMENTS AND OPERATE ON CONSENSUS

STORE OF VALUE

Definition (defined here): A Store of Value[11] is an asset that maintains its value; is based on an agreement[12]: harmony of opinion, action, or character; and consensus[13]: group solidarity in sentiment and belief that something has value.

"Inherent Store of Value" exists when at least two parties agree that a Store of Value has a value and operates on that consensus. One party is willing to sell or trade, and one party is willing to buy or trade; or one party is willing to accept that Store of Value in exchange for another Store of Value (For example, but not limited to: asset to asset, asset to product, asset to service, product to service, service to service, product to

---

[11] "Store of Value" https://www.investopedia.com/terms/s/storeofvalue.asp (accessed December 13, 2018)

[12] "Agreement" harmony of opinion, action, or character https://www.merriam-webster.com/dictionary/agreement (accessed October 7, 2018)

[13] "Consensus" group solidarity in sentiment and belief. https://www.merriam-webster.com/dictionary/consensus (accessed October 7, 2018)

product, legal instrument to product, etc.) It could be U.S. Dollars, gold, a bearer bond, an equity share, coconuts, or Bitcoin.

The incumbent definition of a Store of Value[14] is challenged here. The incumbent definition suggests that a Store of Value should have solid matter longevity. Regardless of its state of solidity; some digital, perishable, intangible, assets; products; instruments; or services may be worth more than gold. For example, in some ecosystems, shark fin can be worth more than gold, and can be exchanged as a valuable Store of Value. A Store of Value is valued by two or more parties who agree in consensus. Certain micro economies might agree that a Store of Value is priced at a certain level because its perceived or actual value in that community is high. Perhaps because, but not limited to, it is culturally significant, has utility, or for philosophical reasons. Perhaps that same Store of Value in another community might be diminished or have no value at all.

A Store of Value is based on an agreement and consensus that something has value. A Store of Value is the manifestation of an agreement and consensus of at least two parties that something has value.

A Store of Value has inherent value in an open market, regardless of the value of the underlying economy, asset, commodity, product, or service. The inherent value of a Store of Value is calculated by its value in an open market at the precise moment that an exchange occurs for another Store of Value, even if the Store of Value consensus is limited to just two parties. A Store of Value shifts in value based on its value in an open

---

[14] "Store of Value" https://www.investopedia.com/terms/s/storeofvalue.asp (accessed December 13, 2018)

market. A Store of Value's value is determined against another Store of Value. For example. Dollars against Euros, Dollars against gold, Dollars against Bitcoin, Dollars against coconuts, equities against Euros, a service against silver, or Yuan against shark fin.

This is true across, within, and outside geo-political sovereign borders and Digital Borders[15], Incumbent and Digital Economies.

---

[15] "Digital Border(s)" This term is created here in this writing to describe the external border between a blockchain, digital ledger, a distributed ledger, versus the outside of the "technical border" of the digital ledger, distributed ledger, or blockchain. A transfer could be executed to a different blockchain, digital ledger, distributed ledger, exchange, wallet, or silo outside of its own native blockchain.

CHAPTER 5

ASSETS, DIGITAL ASSETS, AND DIGITAL UNITS

ASSET

Definition (defined here): An Asset is something of value; and can be, but not necessarily, a Store of Value.

"Something of value" can take many forms. In the Incumbent Economy, assets can be tangible or intangible[16]. For example, tangible Assets include homes, cars, gold, and the paper or coin form of United States Dollars. Intangible Assets include intellectual property, a share of a fund or entity, goodwill, virtual[17], digital[18], a bank's ledger entry, or an idea. In the Digital Economy assets are only digital and virtual and may represent tangible or intangible underlying assets.

An asset can be valuable to one party or more. A Store of Value has value because at least two parties agree it has value.

A Store of Value is the manifestation of an agreement and consensus of at least two parties that something has value.

---

[16] "Intangible" something that may exist but cannot be touched.
[17] "Virtual" being on or simulated on a computer or computer network; relating to, or being a hypothetical particle whose existence is inferred from indirect evidence https://www.merriam-webster.com/dictionary/virtual (accessed October 20, 2018)
[18] "Digital" related to digits composed of data in the form of especially binary digits; characterized by electronic and especially computerized technology https://www.merriam-webster.com/dictionary/digital (accessed October 20, 2018)

DIGITAL ASSET

Definition: Digital is related to digits characterized by computerized technology.

The property and characteristic of Digital Asset technological form: as being "digital" can be compared to the physical property of Incumbent Asset form: as being tangible or intangible.

Definition (defined here) A Digital Asset is something of value where its form is manifest[19] through computer technology.

For example, the United States Dollar manifests in many forms: gold, metal, paper, and digital. Digital forms of the U.S. Dollar are transmitted every day through payment processors and financial institutions. The form that a U.S. Dollar takes in those instances is a binary set of digits on a digital ledger transmitted as packets of data. When a U.S. Dollar is transacted in this way, it is a Digital Asset: "*something of value where its form is manifest through computer technology.*"

A Digital Asset can be valuable to just one party, or as an Inherent Store of Value when at least two parties agree in consensus that the Digital Asset has value.

For example, when Satoshi Nakamoto created Bitcoin, the Digital Asset created in that moment was valuable to just Nakamoto. That Bitcoin created was something of value where its form is manifest through computer technology.

Digital Assets are more than just computer software technology.

---

[19] "Manifest" easily understood or recognized by the mind https://www.merriam-webster.com/dictionary/manifested (accessed October 20, 2018)

When Nakamoto paid for the legendary pizza with Bitcoin[20], the first known official exchange of Bitcoin for product, Bitcoin became an Inherent Store of Value, because at that moment at least two parties agreed that Bitcoin had value equal to the value of one pizza (in context the trading pair was Bitcoin/Pizza). As a result, the transaction was completed, and Bitcoin was exchanged for a pizza.

While Digital Asset form of tangibility is digital and virtual; it is an asset (considered valuable by one or more parties) or a Store of Value (considered valuable by two or more parties) when its perceived market value apart from its physical property is manifest through agreement and consensus by two or more parties. This is what distinguishes a Digital Asset from a mere piece of software.

> *Definition (defined here): A Digital Asset is distinguished from a mere piece of software by a perceived market value as an asset by at least one party, or as a Store of Value by two or more parties.*

A Digital Asset's perceived value as an "Asset" is what distinguishes it from another piece of software. Without at least one party's perception that the Digital software has inherent value, it is reduced to just being Digital, and simply just a piece of computer software.

DIGITAL UNIT

There are components of computer software that do not have financial value and have function or usefulness. The collective narrative about blockchain, digital ledger,

---

[20] See https://blog.blockchain.com/2016/07/13/famous-bitcoin-transactions-the-stories-behind-them (accessed October 20, 2018)

and Digital Asset technologies has adopted the usage term "utility token" to describe these software components offering function and usefulness outside of any financial value. However, the term *"utility token"* is not an appropriate usage of the two individual words within that term to properly define the descriptive intent behind the common usage of the term.

The words token and asset are associated with financial and economic value and not all digital ledger components have inherent, intrinsic, associative financial or economic value.

Economic value can be extracted from utility, usefulness, and function. It is a different analysis from a financial analysis and the metrics are not the same. Financial value, as the concept is presented here for context, operates as a representation of its financial market value in an exchange for other stores of value.

The term "Digital Unit" is a more effective term than the term "Utility Token" to describe software components/items utilized by digital ledgers with function and usefulness that do not have financial value.

The term *"utility"* **as defined by Merriam-Webster**[21] **implies value, economic value, and financial value.**

> *"noun: 1: fitness for some purpose or worth to some end, 2: something useful or designed for use, 3: a service (such as light, power, or water) provided by a public utility, 2: equipment or a piece of equipment to provide such service or a comparable service, 4: a program or routine designed to perform or facilitate especially routine operations (such as copying files or editing text) on a*

---

[21] https://www.merriam-webster.com/dictionary/utility (accessed December 28, 2018)

computer, adjective: 1: capable of serving as a substitute in various roles or positions a utility infielder, 2: kept to provide a useful product or service, 3: serving primarily for utility rather than beauty, 4: designed or adapted for general use a utility tool, 5: of or relating to a utility a utility company."

The term "token" as defined by Merriam-Webster[22] implies value or financial value.

> *"noun: 1a: a piece resembling a coin issued for use (as for fare on a bus) by a particular group on specified terms, b: a piece resembling a coin issued as money by some person or body other than a de jure government, c: a unit of a cryptocurrency Bitcoin tokens, 2: an outward sign or expression 3 : symbol, emblem, b: an instance of a linguistic expression 4: a small part representing the whole c: something given or shown as a guarantee (as of authority, right, or identity) 5: a member of a group (such as a minority) that is included within a larger group through tokenism especially : a token employee 6: distinguishing feature, adjective: 1: representing no more than a symbolic effort by serving or intended to show absence of discrimination, 2: done or given as a token especially in partial fulfillment of an obligation or engagement a token payment."*

Digital Unit

> *Definition (defined here): A piece of software that is functional and useful, is not an asset, has no inherent financial value, external financial value, and does not represent an asset or a store of value that has financial value. It could be fungible or non-fungible depending on its use case. The supply of the software could be finite or infinite depending on its use case. The software can be a manifestation of something, or represent something underlying that may, or may not, have utilitarian or economic value; however, the unit itself has no financial value.*

---

[22] https://www.merriam-webster.com/dictionary/token (accessed December 28, 2018)

Examples: A Vote, Identity, Digital Container, Measurement, Store of Information, or Store of Data.

The term "digital" is defined as:

Definition: Related to digits as characterized by computer technology.

The term "unit" as defined by Merriam-Webster:

"noun" 1a: the first and least natural number, b: a single quantity regarded as a whole in calculation, 2: a determinate quantity, 3: a single thing, person, or group that is a constituent of a whole, 4: a piece or complex of apparatus serving to perform one particular function, adjective: 1: being, relating to, or measuring one unit."

MONEY

Definition (defined here): Money is a generic term which applies to any Store of Value that can be exchanged.

Money can be in the form of a commodity, Digital Commodity, currency, Digital Currency, Digital Certificate of Value, equity, Digital Equity, and any tangible or intangible item. Currency is one form of Money.

MONEY VERSUS TRANSACTIONS OR PAYMENTS

Money is a Store of Value that can be exchanged and is different from a transaction or payment.

The definition of "transaction":

Definition (defined here): A Transaction can be both a process and/or a record. A Transaction is distinct from a Payment. A Transaction can be: 1. an operation to transport, process, record; and 2. a representation or record of digital or analog data, information, financial, tangible, intangible asset transfer (credit, debit, data); or Payment.

The definition of "payment":

Definition (defined here): A Payment is distinct from a transaction. It is the record of exchange of an asset (tangible, intangible, fungible, non-fungible, fiat, digital), other kind of asset, product, or service exchanged for an asset (tangible, intangible, fungible, non-fungible, fiat, digital), other kind of asset, product, or service.

For example, a Store of Value that can be exchanged (Money), can be used to make a record of exchange of assets, products or services for other assets, products, or services (Payment), by initiating a process and record of the financial entry (Transaction).

CHAPTER 6

ECONOMIES

ECONOMIES ARE AGREEMENTS THAT OPERATE ON CONSENSUS

ECONOMY

Definition: An Economy is an area of production, consumption, and trade.[23]

Prior to widespread use of the internet and emergence of Digital Asset technologies, the Incumbent Economy[24] evolved from a collective of small tribes and agrarian societies limited by their geographic boundaries, to the centrally controlled geo-political sovereigns of the world. The internet and Digital Asset technologies challenge the existing construct of centrally controlled geo-political sovereign economies that collectively make up the world's economy.

The internet and Digital Asset technologies create mini economic ecosystems that are not limited to geo-political boundaries. This forces the re-examination of the word "economy". Now the "area" of production, consumption, and trade is not limited

---

[23] "Economy" https://en.wikipedia.org/wiki/Economy/ (Accessed October 4, 2018)
[24] "Incumbent Economy" The economic ecosystem of production, consumption and trade without Digital Assets operating as Stores of Value, utility or function.

to geo-political boundaries. The Digital Economy challenges the current world economic construct through the notion of what constitutes "an area of production, consumption and trade".

> *The Digital Economy offers opportunities for micro-economies to exist that transcend geo-political boundaries in an ecosystem of peer-to-peer engagement through technological innovation.*

ECONOMIES ARE AGREEMENTS

The definition of Agreement according to Merriam-Webster[25]:

> *Agreement noun 1: harmony of opinion, action, or character. 2a: an arrangement as to a course of action reached an agreement as to how to achieve their goal. b: compact, treaty a trade agreement. 3a: a contract duly executed and legally binding, b: the language or instrument embodying such a contract.*

An agreement is the trigger for a transaction which must result in consensus to complete and continue a seamless operation and function. Breakdown in any part of that process results in a failure for that agreement to process, complete, and become a permanent record in the ecosystem.

> *Agreement > Transaction > Consensus = Completion and Recording of the Transaction.*

Economies are ecosystems of agreement and operate because the parties agree about the value, nature, structure, and parameter of an interaction. Where there is no agreement, there is no interaction or a trigger for a transaction, and it fails.

---

[25] "Agreement" https://www.merriam-webster.com/dictionary/agreement (accessed October 7, 2018)

For example; First, two parties, a buyer and seller meet and agree on a price for a product. Second, the buyer usually offers some version of money in exchange for the product. Third, the buyer agrees to pay the amount and nature of agreed upon tender[26] to the seller for the product. Fourth, the transaction is triggered. Fifth, the seller and the buyer are in consensus about the terms of the agreement and the transfer exchange. Sixth, the buyer presents the money, and the seller accepts the money. Seventh, the seller transfers the product, and buyer accepts the product. Eighth, the exchange is completed and recorded.

ECONOMIES OPERATE ON CONSENSUS

The definition of Consensus according to Merriam-Webster[27]:

> *"Consensus noun, often attributive 1: general agreement. 2: group solidarity in sentiment and belief."*

Consensus is the collective agreement (the result of a moment of collective agreement) between parties. In the Incumbent Economy consensus is demonstrated by, but not limited to, an executed contract, handshake, an act of exchange or delivery, and results as an entry into a ledger.

In the Digital Economy, blockchain transaction technology is automated to process transactions arising out of an agreement to arrive at consensus.

---

[26] "Tender" noun (1), often attributive 1 : an unconditional offer of money or service in satisfaction of a debt or obligation made to save a penalty or forfeiture for nonpayment or nonperformance 2 : an offer or proposal made for acceptance: such as a : an offer of a bid for a contract b : tender offer 3 : something that may be offered in payment specifically : money https://www.merriam-webster.com/dictionary/tender (accessed October 11. 2018)

[27] "Consensus" https://www.merriam-webster.com/dictionary/consensus (accessed October 7, 2018)

An agreement triggers the transaction, the computers process the transaction, and when consensus is reached by the Blockchain Nodes[28], the result is recorded. In the Digital Economy as it operates today, consensus is arrived through the process of algorithmic[29] cryptographic[30] technology. Computers and algorithms process an agreement which initiates a transaction that results in the automation and a journey to arrive to the point of consensus. Consensus is automated and completed by the Blockchain Nodes and are the automated version of an Incumbent Economy's handshake. The incumbent handshake is equal to the moment of computed Blockchain Node consensus, the incumbent physical transfer is the electronic exchange, and the written entry into the ledger is the permanent record on the digital ledger.

This process is just like the process in the Incumbent Economy…except it is automated, and the record is immutable[31].

Agreement > Transaction > Consensus = Completion and Permanent Recording of the Transaction

INCUMBENT ECONOMY VERSUS DIGITAL ECONOMY

The Incumbent Economy is a collection of sovereign micro economies with geo-political micro economic borders. The Digital Economy has different micro economic borders. "Digital Borders"[32].

---

[28] "Blockchain Node" A computer in a blockchain (https://www.investopedia.com/terms/b/blockchain.asp/ (accessed October 2, 2018)
[29] "Algorithm" A step-by-step procedure for solving a problem or accomplishing some end https://www.merriam-webster.com/dictionary/algorithm/ (accessed October 2, 2018)
[30] "Cryptographic" Of, relating to, or using cryptography https://www.merriam-webster.com/dictionary/cryptographic/ (accessed October 2, 2018)
[31] "Immutable" Not capable of or susceptible to change https://www.merriam-webster.com/dictionary/immutable (accessed October 2, 2018)

Defining the Digital Economy
Lori Jo Underhill

The definition of Digital Economy:

Definition (defined here): The "Digital Economy" is an ecosystem of production, consumption, trade transcending geo-political boundaries where "Digital Assets" operate in a virtual or digital environment as Stores of Value, utility, function where there is agreement and consensus about the value of the Digital Assets exchanged in the ecosystem and the method of transfer between them.

Economies now operate both on a macro level across (Incumbent) geo-political sovereign borders or across Digital Borders, or on a micro level within geo-political sovereign borders and within Digital Borders. Currently the Incumbent Economy and the Digital Economy can interact with each other through exchanges and commerce where assets from both economies can be transacted and exchanged.

The Incumbent Economy now has a powerful example of a consortium that extends beyond one geo-political border. The European Union has demonstrated that the use of a singular currency beyond a singular geo-political territory is possible. This model can be examined as the start of the trend toward consortiums of communities with shared purpose and cultural values that band together in monetary policy. Digital Economies are of similar character to the European Union. Participants of Digital Economies come together in agreement and consensus about the structure, nature, and method of its monetary policy through a common cause of culture, values, and purpose.

---

[32] "Digital Border(s)" This term is created here in this writing to describe the external border between a blockchain, digital ledger, a distributed ledger, versus the outside of the "technical border" of the digital ledger, distributed ledger, or blockchain. A transfer could be executed to a different blockchain, digital ledger, distributed ledger, exchange, wallet, or silo outside of its own native blockchain.

Digital Economies are formed out of philosophical, functional, utilitarian, economic, or cultural agreements between parties, and operate in consensus for transactioning with others who share those same philosophies, values, or needs.

Opinion: As of the date of this writing, the choice to participate in these economies is generally voluntary for most world citizens who have access to the technologies. However, some geo-political sovereigns, have banned the use of Digital Currency.[33] This circumstance may change and shift as geo-political sovereigns begin to embrace these technologies and adopt them as fiat[34]. In that circumstance, the geo-political economic border, and the digital economic border will merge.

The Digital Economy offers opportunities for micro-economies to exist that transcend geo-political boundaries in an ecosystem of peer-to-peer engagement through technological innovation. Upon adoption of these technologies by geo-political sovereigns, or consortiums of multiple geo-political sovereigns, the geo-political border, economic border, and Digital Border will synchronize.[35]

ECONOMIES VERSUS MARKETS

Economies are ecosystems of production, consumption, trade and are based on agreement and consensus. Markets are the microcosm of just the trade portion of the

---

[33] See https://www.investopedia.com/articles/forex/041515/countries-where-bitcoin-legal-illegal.asp (accessed October 19, 2018)

[34] "fiat" an authoritative or arbitrary order : "decree government by fiat" https://www.merriam-webster.com/dictionary/fiat (accessed September 22, 2018)

[35] In Venezuela, the geo-political sovereign government introduced the "Petro", a Digital Currency backed by oil, because its native fiat tender had reduced in value, and trust and confidence had almost completely diminished. See https://www.washingtonpost.com/news/worldviews/wp/2018/02/20/venezuela-launches-the-petro-its-cryptocurrency/?noredirect=on&utm_term=.9ea9170d8dd8 (accessed October 15, 2018)

economy, as a point of exchange of one Store of Value for another Store of Value. Some markets are specialized. The regulated New York Stock Exchange is a market for regulated equities (shares of ownership of regulated entities). The Grand Bazaar in Istanbul is an economy. There is production (making of food, products, and services), consumption (eating or consuming of food, products, or services), and trade (microcosm (individual booths) of markets of Stores of Value for food, products, or services).

Digital Assets and Incumbent Assets can be exchanged on a peer-to-peer basis (in unregulated markets without third-party involvement) within digital or geo-political sovereign borders (inside the micro economy), or beyond digital or geo-political sovereign borders (outside of its micro economy). If holders of those assets meet, agree in consensus, and create a way to exchange the assets without third-party involvement; the method of exchange is exactly like the exchange of assets and commodities (dollars for bananas) at the local Piggly Wiggly Supermarket or the General Store on Mainstreet.

CHAPTER 7

INCUMBENT ASSETS VERSUS DIGITAL ASSETS

Digital Asset and Digital Unit Fundamentals

Digital Assets have financial value in addition to, outside of, or concurrent with function and usefulness. This value is proven through agreement and consensus between parties in an open market. A Digital Asset is distinguished from a Digital Unit which has function and usefulness but no financial value as an Asset, Store of Value, or medium of exchange; either within or outside of its own economy and/or Digital Border.

A fundamental Digital Asset contextual framework (taxonomy) must be constructed by first determining the foundational base characteristic nature of each asset. Digital Units are not Digital Assets and as a result have a distinct set of evaluation characteristics.

A deep study of over 2500 Digital Assets confirmed the following foundational characteristics appropriate to evaluate Digital Assets:

1. Physical form, property, or tangibility.

2. The nature of its fungibility or non-fungibility.

3. Whether the Digital Asset represents an underlying asset either unique or fungible.

4. Whether the Digital Asset is supported by, is the native tender of, or utilized by an underlying economy, technology, or utility.

5. Whether the Digital Asset is a representation of an underlying asset or an asset unto itself.

6. Whether the Digital Asset's supply is finite, or the asset is created as needed by its economy or utility.

7. Whether the Digital Asset has financial value both within and outside of its own economy or ecosystem.

Technology, utility, features, and use cases change or become obsolete; therefore, are not a functional basis characteristic to create a proper taxonomy.

> *Digital Commodities, Digital Currencies, Digital Certificates of Value, Digital Equities, and Digital Units all operate on a digital ledger, distributed ledger, or blockchain. This broad technological characteristic does not distinguish one from another. Digital ledger transactioning technology or other technologies are not a sufficient basis to determine a classification and characterization standard. The evaluation to consider a technology feature is a second level analysis.*

This distinctive insight uncovered through this research is what distinguishes these findings and the DASH taxonomy from any other known attempts to classify and categorize exchange traded Digital Assets. The focus on technology and use case is a reason for other failed attempts.

Algorithmic[36] and cryptographic[37] transactioning technologies for digital ledgers can vary; and do not offer a properly distinguished, delineated, scalable, coherent mechanism to analyze and determine fundamental parallels or distinctions between Digital Assets and Digital Units for extensible characterization, classification, and contextual purposes.

An algorithm technology or a nuanced benefit from a transaction technology capability generally serves more as a feature, than a proper fundamental classification and characterization standard. However, if a Digital Asset's transactioning method or technology is novel, adds measurable uniqueness, enhanced functionality, or financial value; the value-add technology or method could offer an enhanced underlying value proposition possibly distinguishing the Digital Asset from another within or outside of its own asset class.

For example, if a Digital Asset utilizes the same transactioning algorithm as Bitcoin[38], but also utilizes an additional network layer enhancement protocol which adds a feature such as cyber security or function such as authentication, the protocol would then offer an enhancement or distinction to the basic transaction technology utilized by many Digital Assets across the economy. The cyber security feature may be enough to

---

[36] "Algorithm" A step-by-step procedure for solving a problem or accomplishing some end https://www.merriam-webster.com/dictionary/algorithm/ (accessed October 2, 2018)

[37] "Cryptographic" Of, relating to, or using cryptography https://www.merriam-webster.com/dictionary/cryptographic/ (accessed October 2, 2018)

[38] Bitcoin utilizes Hashcash "Like many cryptographic algorithms hashcash uses a hash function as a building block, in the same way that HMAC, or RSA signatures are defined on a pluggable hash-function (commonly denoted by the naming convention of algorithm-hash: HMAC-SHA1, HMAC-MD5, HMAC-SHA256, RSA-SHA1, etc), hashcash can be instantiated with different functions, hashcash-SHA1 (original), hashcash-SHA256^2 (bitcoin), hashcash. (litecoin)." https://en.bitcoin.it/wiki/Hashcash (accessed September 30, 2018)

enhance the Digital Asset's primary value proposition (or marketability) enough to distinguish it from another Digital Asset and serve as a consideration in determining the economic sector where it functions and operates.

Digital Asset Construct Analysis

1. The first step to create a Digital Asset taxonomy includes the identification of the proper foundational characteristics and defining the Digital Asset classes by 1. testing against the root foundational attributes, 2. evaluating the similarities and distinctions, and 3. separating by asset class.

2. The second step requires an evaluation of the function, use case, technology, primary purpose, economic revenue sector, or attributes that create parallels and distinctions between assets within the same asset class.

This step determines sub-asset classes or separates assets by economic sector. The outcome is demonstrated in the current implementation of the DASH that is combined with exchange traded market data, creating the first total market and economic sector indices. This work is visualized on CoinSector.[39] These attributes can also be tested against Digital Assets not traded on third party exchanges. This level will further reveal the proper agency for regulatory oversight.

3. Finally, the evaluation of the use case, technology, and applicability under current law is done at the third level. This will determine the applicable rules to evaluate each Digital Asset's use case and function. Determinations based on issues include, but are not limited to custody, where the Digital Assets are exchanged, terms for any

---

[39] https://www.coinsector.io

investment contract or profit generation implementation on the Digital Ledger, to name a few.

A focus on the fundamental characteristics of Digital Assets proves that Digital Assets cannot convert. For example, from a Digital Equity to a Digital Currency. These fundamental distinctions prevent a shift in a Digital Asset's classification. Digital Equities can be Stores of Value or mediums of exchange in the same way that Digital Currencies can be Stores of Value or mediums of exchange. Digital Assets are Stores of Value and can be exchanged; however, this fact alone does not shift the nature of their fundamental characteristics or change all Digital Assets into Digital Currencies.

Incumbent Assets do not morph in the incumbent and tangible world, they do not change. Digital Assets do not morph, they do not change. Assets are either fungible or non-fungible. A non-fungible equity cannot change into a fungible currency.

Opinion: Determining the appropriate regulatory oversight and classification for any asset should be based on factors such as: an analysis of the asset's physical properties, supply, where and how it operates; where the asset is held or controlled, if through custodianship; where and how it is exchanged; the purpose it serves in any underlying economy other than its value as an Inherent Store of Value on third party financial exchanges; and what physical, technological, or utilization enhancements or inherent properties it has. These characteristics or methods of exchange should be considered by regulators in determining which Digital Assets are regulated, taxed, controlled, and under what authority, exactly like assets operating in the Incumbent Economy.

For example, below is a comparison between an asset in the Incumbent Economy versus a Digital Asset in the Digital Economy:

In the Incumbent Economy, the U.S. Dollar in the form of tangible paper, coin, financial instruments, operating within and outside of its own micro economy (the United States geo-political border), is physically traded in tangible form both within its own economy and outside of its economy (in open markets), sometimes through electronic transfers, as a Store of Value, and does not have any additional inherent technology or utility capability other than being a form of money. The U.S. Dollar can manifest in tangible, paper and coin, and intangible form, through entries on ledgers, payment processing, and custodians, and does not have an official fiat[40] fungible digital asset version of itself, although in some instances, the U.S. Dollar is converted into digital form for purposes of transmission and custody.

In the Digital Economy, Storj is a Digital Currency in the form of a Digital Asset, operating within and outside of its own micro economy (the Storj technical blockchain Digital Border). Storj is traded electronically both within and outside of its own micro-economy (in open markets) as a Store of Value and has a technological feature or utility capability other than a form of money. Storj is "a protocol that creates a distributed network for the formation and execution of storage contracts between peers. The Storj protocol enables peers on the network to negotiate contracts, transfer data, verify the integrity and availability of remote data, retrieve data, and pay other

---

[40] "fiat" fiat noun "1 : a command or act of will that creates something without or as if without further effort According to the Bible, the world was created by fiat. 2 : an authoritative. https://www.merriam-webster.com/dictionary/fiat/ (accessed September 22, 2018)

nodes. Each peer is an autonomous agent, capable of performing these actions without significant human interaction."[41] Storj is the native Digital Asset (the blockchain's native tender) of its underlying economy (the Storj blockchain). Storj is a Digital Asset and does not have a tangible version of itself.

STORES OF VALUE AND FINANCIAL INSTRUMENTS
COMMODITIES

Commodities are Inherent Stores of Value and result from agreement and consensus. Commodities operate as a Store of Value beyond the borders of an underlying micro economy, such as a geo-political sovereignty (state or country) or an underlying economic ecosystem (for example, a barter system, or a Digital Economy such as a blockchain).

In the Incumbent Economy, commodities are generally considered Stores of Value both within and outside geo-political sovereign borders. A commodity traded on an open market has inherent value, because its value stands on its own without an underlying economy, and there are at least two parties in agreement in consensus that the commodity has value. Generally, commodities can be traded within and across both geo-political and Digital Borders, as markets exist in agreement and consensus about its inherent value.

---

[41] Quoted from "Storj Whitepaper" Section 2 Design https://storj.io/storj.pdf/ (accessed September 30, 2018)

DIGITAL COMMODITY

Definition (defined here): A "Digital Commodity" is a consensus of trust and confidence; its value exists on its own without an underlying economy. A Digital Commodity can be perceived to be scarce, in limited supply, difficult or expensive to divide, extract, use, or transfer. A Digital Commodity is fungible. Fungible assets are not unique to one another, are the same in character, and are interchangeable.

For example. One bar of 24-carat gold is the same as another bar of 24-carat gold. One Bitcoin is the same as another Bitcoin in its character. A relative framework for comparison in the Incumbent Economy is a tangible commodity; such as gold, silver, or pork bellies. Inherent value exists on its own within a market to value and trade the asset for other items of value.

At some point in human history, the world agreed in consensus that gold has value. Gold is traded within and outside micro economies. Now the world has agreed that Bitcoin has value. Bitcoin is traded within and outside micro economies.

In general, commodities (tangible, intangible, and Digital Commodities) are not optimized for payment transactioning. For example, imagine trying to buy a Lamborghini with bars of gold. One might be able to execute that transaction, but the transaction cost is likely high, conversion may be slow, and the process might be tedious. The dealer will have to physically move the gold around, possibly test the gold, and find a market to sell it to convert it to a more effective payment medium (likely an accepted fungible currency) to transact his business, pay the manufacturer, and his vendors.

Intangible and Digital Commodities are similar in character to tangible commodities. They have value within and outside the micro economy.

Policy Opinion[42]: In the United States, commodity futures are traded through regulated products (for example, exchange traded funds, custodial transactions) in regulated markets are regulated by the Commodity Futures Trading Commission (CFTC). Based on the characteristics of these assets, tangible, intangible, and Digital Commodities traded as a part of regulated financial instruments in financial markets should be regulated under this authority. Commodities traded for other Stores of Value in an open peer-to-peer market (for example, at the general store) and not in regulated markets should not be regulated. That is, peer-to-peer transactions.

CURRENCIES

A currency is distinguished from a commodity through support or value within or from an underlying economy. The currency's inherent value on the open market, may have little to do with its value, or the number of participants in the underlying economy where it can also be utilized as a Store of Value, utility, enhancement, function, or technology to the underlying economy.

INCUMBENT CURRENCIES

The definition of fiat according to Merriam-Webster[43]:

> *"fiat noun 1: a command or act of will that creates something without or as if without further effort According to the Bible, the world was created by fiat. 2: an authoritative*

---

[42] Note: The policy opinions in this paper are presented with examples in the United States, although could apply to any geo-political construct already in place in other jurisdictions. Jurisdictions without existing regulating bodies could use the recommendations as a basis for guidance toward future frameworks for oversight.

[43] "fiat" https://www.merriam-webster.com/dictionary/fiat (accessed September 22, 2018)

determination: dictate a fiat of conscience. 3: an authoritative or arbitrary order: decree government by fiat."

The world currently refers to the currency of the Incumbent Economy as a tender or financial instrument supported by a geo-political sovereign governance and economy; and is usually referred to, and commonly known as, "fiat currency" operating under, in decree from, within, and possibly outside a sovereign geo-political border.

Geo-political sovereigns are the micro economies operating within the worldwide Incumbent economic ecosystem. Worldwide fiat currencies in the Incumbent Economy are generally the legal tender of the underlying economy of the sovereign which supports the currency. For example, the United States U.S. Dollar (USD) or the European Union EURO (EUR) as legal tender.

To transact fiat currency within a geo-political sovereign economy, generally one must convert another Store of Value to the fiat currency of the economy where one wishes to transact.

An individual with U.S. Dollars, upon travel to the European Union, will likely have to convert U.S. Dollars to Euros to effectively and efficiently transact there at the lowest possible cost.

Some currencies are Inherent Stores of Value beyond the borders of the geo-political sovereignty supporting it. The U.S. Dollar has markets throughout the world where it can be exchanged for other currencies and commodities in addition to its value in the United States economy within its geo-political sovereign border.

Defining the Digital Economy
Lori Jo Underhill

Not all geo-political sovereign fiat currencies are Inherent Stores of Value outside of their own economies. For example. At the time of this writing, the Venezuelan Bolivar currency is losing value within and outside of its own economy. The currency is a Store of Value within its micro economy operating within its own geo-political sovereign border, but outside of its border, its Store of Value is largely diminished, and possibly has no value beyond its own geo-political sovereign border.

DIGITAL CURRENCIES

Digital Currency is like fiat currency in that it has some operative value within its underlying economy, generally serving as the underlying economy's native and most widely accepted transaction and/or payment tender (term of art offered for context), and Store of Value creating or transferring value within the underlying economy. Similarly, it may, or may not, have any value outside of the underlying economy, and is fungible.

Distinctively, fiat currency generally has limiting use as only a Store of Value transaction and/or payment tender. Digital Currency offers further value in its capacity to offer enhanced economic value through function, utility, or technology in addition to serving as its native transactional payment tender and Store of Value. This multi-use function and/or utility characteristic capability within, and possibly outside, of its own blockchain, distributed ledger, digital ledger, or interledger connected economy, is the most difficult for people to grasp and the major distinction between Incumbent (fiat) versus Digital Currency. However, not all Digital Currency has multi-characteristic value.

Defining the Digital Economy
Lori Jo Underhill

Blockchains and Digital Ledgers are the transactional areas and operational basis for the micro economies operating in the worldwide Digital Economy. Blockchains and Digital Ledgers are the "area sovereigns" (term of art offered for context) governing the transactional terms and parameters for the Digital Currencies accepted within their underlying economies, exactly the way fiat currencies operate within their economies.

The value of a Digital Currency within its own micro Digital Economy also causes confusion, as its value could be derived from one or more financial, economic, functional, utilitarian, and technological characteristic. For example, in addition to operating as a transaction and/or payment tender and Store of Value, a Digital Currency could function as an envelope that delivers digital content; serve as a payment Store of Value within its own economy; deliver transaction information from one point to another; represent reward points; serve as a digital vote in an election; represent a measure of solar energy; operate as a data reference store; offer a technology enhancement; be an interledger protocol; be a cybersecurity technology; transmit internet of things or geolocation data points from one place to another; or allow a transaction in a bumble bee or cannabis ecosystem, etc.

On the date of this writing, there were over 1500 Digital Currencies operating within their own economies worldwide in 24 economic sectors, and over 250 subsectors. These currencies are both Inherent Stores of Value on open exchange traded markets, and offer financial, economic, or utilitarian value within the underlying micro economies where they operate.

This is the most important characteristic of a Digital Currency. Distinct from a fiat currency, a Digital Currency is a Store of Value within its own economy, with characteristic potential to offer financial, utilitarian, functional, or technological value within its own micro economy, and possibly beyond its own economy, apart from operating as the native transactional and/or payment tender of its micro economy.

Digital Currencies are distinctive from Digital Units in that Digital Currencies have financial value within, and possibly outside, of their underlying economies; where Digital Units do not have financial value, having only functional or utilitarian value; which arguably could be measured as economic value using different metrics, an analysis outside the scope of this writing.

Opinion: This is the far-reaching value of the Digital Economy.

DIGITAL CURRENCY

Definition (defined here): A "Digital Currency" requires a consensus of trust, confidence; is a unit of account, divisible, stable, accepted; measured against other assets or currencies of value; possibly regulated by authority or governance framework; and supported by an underlying technology, utility, activity, or economy. It may have value or utility within its underlying micro economy; and may, or may not, have any value outside of the underlying economy. Currencies are generated or destroyed as needed for utilization by the underlying economy by the authority or governance framework. Currencies are fungible. Fungible assets are not unique to one another, are the same in character, and are interchangeable.

As fungible assets are exchanged, one equals another in character[44]. For example, one U.S. Dollar is the same as another U.S. Dollar. One Ether is the same as another Ether in its character.

---

[44] Value of fungible assets is determined by many factors and is outside of the scope of this

In addition, the assignment of the particular fungible asset to a custodial party is inconsequential. In other words, it does not matter who holds or possesses a particular asset of identical characteristics or class. These assets are not unique to one another.

To transact Digital Currency within the micro Digital Economy, generally one must convert an Inherent Store of Value or asset to the currency of the micro economy (blockchain or digital ledger community) where the party wishes to transact.

For example, if a party wishes to transact within the Ethereum Blockchain economy, the party will have to convert an asset, U.S. Dollar, Euro, Bitcoin, or Dash to Ether (ETH) to effectively and efficiently transact within the Ethereum Blockchain at the lowest possible cost.

A party may take ETH outside of the Ethereum blockchain and trade it on an open market exchange if a market exists in agreement and consensus that ETH is an Inherent Store of Value outside of its Digital Border in its own micro economy (its own blockchain or digital ledger). The value of ETH within its own blockchain and outside of its own blockchain may not be at all related, as the consensus of value of a Digital Currency in exchange traded markets may be affected by market conditions, supply, demand, environment, or sentiment about its value as a valuable asset in the future apart from its value within its own economy.[45] This is exactly how fiat currency operates in the Incumbent Economy.

---

writing.
[45] Value of currencies is determined by many factors and is outside of the scope of this writing.

Not all Digital Currencies are Inherent Stores of Value outside of their own economies.

The participants within a micro economy may be in agreement and consensus about a Digital Currency's financial or economic value, function or utility within its own Digital Border; however, outside of its Digital Border, its financial or economic value as a Store of Value may be largely diminished or non-existent. The Digital Currency may not be available beyond its own Digital Border and may have no value beyond its own Digital Border.[46]

An example of this circumstance would be a Digital Currency sold or gifted to private investors or contributors, but no market exists for it beyond its own Digital Economy, digital ledger, or blockchain ecosystem. Perhaps the currency was sold in an ICO (Initial Coin Offering), the developers gifted the currency to others (Airdrop), or in exchange for resources.

Comparative Use Case: There are Digital Currencies offering Proof of Stake[47] interest for depositing funds into a wallet and holding them for a period. This process compares directly to a deposit account in a banking system, and the characteristics are exactly like an interest-bearing bank account. There are Digital Currencies operating in lending. This process compares directly to a banking function in the United States including payment processing, and financial transactioning.

---

[46] Note: the valuation process to determine an asset's economic value is outside the scope of this writing, as this study is limited to identifying definitions, characteristics, and considerations that affect value.

[47] "Proof of Stake" is a Cryptography algorithm used as a basis for transactioning for some Digital Assets. Further information about this topic can be found here: https://www.investopedia.com/terms/p/proof-stake-pos.asp (accessed September 22, 2018)

Defining the Digital Economy
Lori Jo Underhill

Policy Opinion: In the United States, currencies and banking activities including payments and payment processing are regulated by the U.S. Treasury. Based on the characteristics of these assets, both fiat and Digital Currencies, and any Digital Assets operating in banking like economic activities in the "Financial Transaction" (equal to banks or payment processors) economic sub-sector, or "Crypto Mining" (equal to payment processors) economic sub-sector should be regulated under this authority, with capital requirements, KYC, and AML rules. Next steps for geo-political sovereigns would be to create Digital versions of their fiat legal tenders. Venezuela recently issued the Venezuelan fiat Digital Certificate of Value (defined below), the "Petro."[48] This instrument is backed by oil. When a geo-political sovereign, such as the Venezuelan government, adopts a Digital Currency as its native fiat currency, the new instrument is the 'Digital fiat Currency" of the geo-political sovereign.

DIGITAL CERTIFICATE OF VALUE

Definition (defined here): A "Digital Certificate of Value" has inherent value as a representation of a certificate that can be presented in exchange for the underlying asset (tangible, intangible, Digital Commodity or currency), in proportionate value as identified by the governance of the Digital Asset. Digital Certificates of Value are fungible. Fungible assets are not unique to one another, are the same in character, and are interchangeable.

A relative framework for comparison is a certificate for gold or a certificate for a fiat currency. Inherent value exists on its own within a market to value and trade the asset for other items of value or in exchange for the underlying asset. This distinction is different than an

---

[48] See https://www.washingtonpost.com/news/worldviews/wp/2018/02/20/venezuela-launches-the-petro-its-cryptocurrency/?noredirect=on&utm_term=.9ea9170d8dd8 (accessed October 15, 2018)

asset where its value is "pegged"[49] to an underlying asset. A Certificate of Value can be presented to the sovereign or custodian in exchange for the actual underlying asset.

If a Digital Asset is backed by a fiat currency such as the U.S. Dollar, one may hear the term "Stablecoin" to describe this Digital Asset. These assets may be exchanged for that fiat currency upon demand or an agreed upon store of value according to the underlying governance. This is like the U.S. Dollar before the early 1970's when the dollar was backed by gold.

Policy Opinion: In the United States, currencies and banking activities are regulated by the U.S. Treasury. Based on the characteristics of these assets, both fiat and Digital Currencies, and any Digital Assets operating as fungible Digital Certificates of Value backed by underlying assets should be regulated under the U.S. Treasury as an asset backed currency, like the U.S. Dollar when it was backed by gold.

DIGITAL EQUITY - INSTRUMENTS OF EXCHANGE OR OWNERSHIP

Definition (defined here): A "Digital Equity" is a representation of an ownership interest; whole or fractional, tangible or intangible. A market may or may not exist in consensus for the value of the underlying property. A Digital Equity is difficult or impossible to divide. A Digital Equity is non-fungible. A non-fungible asset is unique in its characteristic as a representation of another asset or item, or the manifestation of one unique and serialized intangible or tangible asset or item. Digital Equities are unique to one another, distinct in character, and not interchangeable.

Examples: Unique Shares of an Entity, Ownership in Real Property, Cryptokitties, Bonds, Shares in Financial Products, Unique

---

[49] "Pegged" verb. to fix or hold (something, such as prices or wage increases) at a predetermined level or rate https://www.merriam-webster.com/dictionary/pegged (accessed October 15, 2016)

Artwork, Jewelry, or Couture Fashion. Any asset that is indivisible, serialized, or unique.

A relative framework for comparison is exchange traded securities, stocks, bonds, deeds of trust, legal ownership documents, agreements, interest bearing assets, equities, ownership for real property, legal, or financial instruments, unique artwork, or even one of a kind garment couture. Inherent value exists on its own within a market to value and trade the asset for other items of value. This class includes but is not limited to Security Tokens and like financial instruments (Bonds, Interest Bearing, Deeds, et all) as determined under law. Digital Equities are non-fungible unique manifested or representative digitized versions of the underlying unique asset.

DIGITAL EQUITIES ARE DISTINCT FROM INCUMBENT STOCK EQUITY INSTRUMENTS

There are three reasons why Digital Equities are distinct from Incumbent Equities.

1. The Digital Equity may or may not be held in custody by a third party and could be held directly by the owner.

2. Serialization, Identity, and Authentication rights are an integral, inherent, and fundamental part of the asset.

3. Digital Assets are generally traded and exchanged in more than one market, not necessarily held in custody by a third party, and the characteristics and material financial and/or economic terms of the asset are not necessarily equal to another Digital

Asset of the same name or symbol at the same moment in time. These characteristics of identity, financial, and economic value are usually distinct and unique.

Opinion: A Digital Equity has unique ownership, identity, and authentication characteristics creating it inherently distinct from any other Digital Asset. These unique qualities add a fundamental attribute characteristically inherent to the Digital Asset. This, coupled with the fact that Digital Equities are not traded in just one market, creates an unequal material financial and/or economic value, further supporting a non-fungible legal determination.

A blockchain or distributed ledger records a transaction for a particular asset. That asset's ownership is determinable through the line of transactions that are immutable, traceable, and identifiable.

Securities law in many jurisdictions strictly require reporting, accountability, place limitations on legal accredited ownership, enforce custodianship rules, and require transparent exchange traceability for purposes of KYC and AML regulations. These requirements render the asset non-fungible by the very nature of its lack of agnostic, non-unique, and non-fluid exchangeability. Digital Equities are distinct from tangible currencies and other tangible assets that can be exchanged and transported entirely outside of electronically traceable conduits, and under certain circumstances do not fall under strict reporting and accountability requirements.

There are three further definitions that should be considered to properly sub-classify Digital Certificates of Value and Digital Equities. An asset classified as a Certificate of Value could be a "Representative Asset" or "Underlying Asset", and a

Defining the Digital Economy
Lori Jo Underhill

Digital Equity could be a "Manifested Asset", "Representative Asset", or "Underlying Asset". Digital Asset sub-classes will further categorize these assets in a naming convention such as: Digital Equity - Entity Security, Digital Equity - Real Estate, Digital Equity - Bond, Digital Equity - Real Property, Digital Equity - Digital Property, etc.

The definition of "Manifested Asset":

Manifested Asset

> *Definition (defined here): A Manifested Asset is a Digital Equity that is a digital non-fungible unique manifestation of a store of value without an underlying asset. These are unique, serialized, and non-fungible assets.*

The definition of "Representative Asset":

Representative Asset

> *Definition (defined here): A Representative Asset is a Digital Asset that is the representation of an underlying fungible or non-fungible asset (tangible, intangible, or digital). Non-fungible as a Digital Equity, and fungible as a Certificate of Value.*

The definition of "Underlying Asset":

Underlying Asset

> *Definition (defined here): An Underlying Asset is an asset (tangible, intangible, or digital) represented by another Digital Asset.*

It is conceivable that it will be determined that a non-fungible Representative Asset can "wrap" a fungible Underlying Asset such as a share of fungible common stock.

Defining the Digital Economy
Lori Jo Underhill

Law is firmly rooted in definition and classification, and this construct supports existing regulatory and financial infrastructures.

Some Digital Equities, but not all, fit the definition of the legal standard issued in the Howey Test[50]. This construct could expand with Digital Asset sub-classes and economic sectors for each specific type of Digital Equity, further identifying the economic sector and industry subsector where Digital Equities operate. For Example: Asset Class: Digital Equity > Sub Asset Class: Digital Stock Equity (or for example, Digital Bonds) > Economic Sector > Economic Subsector > Function > Description. The construct will expand upon the entry of more participants into the category, or upon an asset's status determination under law.

Policy Opinion: In the United States, equities and financial services, such as entities issuing securities, broker/dealers, exchanges, financial services companies issuing exchange traded funds are regulated by the Securities and Exchange Commission (SEC) and Financial Industry Regulatory Authority (FINRA). Based on the characteristics of non-fungible Digital Equities traded on exchanges, which include and are not limited to serialized asset backed equities, asset backed funds shares, activities of Digital Asset broker/dealers, asset custodians of funds, share of non-fungible instruments, and exchange activities from entities operating exchanges in the Financial Exchange economic sub-sector should be regulated under the SEC and FINRA.

New Digital Asset Use Case: Exchanges requiring a buy-in of the exchange's native currency. There is a characteristic unique to some Digital Assets that operate as

---

[50] "The Howey Test" https://supreme.justia.com/cases/federal/us/328/293/#294 (accessed September 22, 2018)

an exchange's native currency. An example of this: The exchange requires a buy-in to a fungible singular currency to trade and exchange for other currencies.

Policy Opinion: The native fungible Digital Asset (Digital Currency of the exchange) should be regulated as a currency under the U.S. Treasury. The underlying exchange activities should be regulated under the SEC and/or FINRA with considerations to whether the exchange operates as a custodian.

New Digital Asset Use Case: Non-fungible non-exchange traded Digital Assets. There is a type of Digital Equity asset which is non-fungible and represent serialized fractional or whole ownership of a unique underlying asset that might not be an exchange traded Digital Asset. This Digital Asset could represent an underlying tangible, intangible, or Digital Asset (for example, a home or artwork). The characteristic that defines these assets is that they are not exchange traded and represent a serialized underlying asset that is unique to itself and is not fungible.

Policy Opinion: In the United States, non-fungible, unique, non-exchange traded Assets are not currently regulated. Assets are defined as "Something with economic value." Non-fungible, non-exchange traded Digital Assets not held in custody, should not be federally regulated. In the United States, states have an interest to regulate real property ownership information for tax and other purposes. Any tangible, intangible, real or Digital Assets that states have an interest in regulating should be evaluated under use case analysis. The process would be to analyze the nature of each asset and any parallels in applicability between the Real Asset use cases currently regulated under law, and the Digital Asset use case versions of these assets. A parallel result would determine that those Digital Assets would fall under regulation at the state level to serve state interests. However, because these non-fungible, unique, non-exchange traded, Digital Assets represent economic value; conceivably, they could be held in custody by a third-party entity. If these non-fungible non-exchange traded assets are held in custody by a third party, they should be regulated by FINRA.

CHAPTER 8

THE NEW DIGITAL ECONOMY SUMMARIZED

The exchange traded Digital Economy is separated into four asset classes.

The DASH™ Digital Asset Sector Hierarchy Framework Digital Asset Class identification analysis considerations, other than as a Store of Value as a Digital Asset traded and exchanged for value in the marketplace are:

1. Physical form, property, or tangibility.

2. The nature of its fungibility or non-fungibility.

3. Whether the Digital Asset represents an underlying asset either unique or fungible.

4. Whether the Digital Asset is supported by, is the native tender of, or utilized by an underlying economy, technology, or utility.

5. Whether the Digital Asset is a representation of an underlying asset or an asset unto itself.

6. Whether the Digital Asset's supply is finite, or the asset is created as needed by its economy or utility.

7. Whether the Digital Asset has financial value both within and outside of its own economy or ecosystem.

Defining the Digital Economy
Lori Jo Underhill

For regulatory and tax purposes, considerations are: where the asset is exchanged, if held in custody or by the owner, and terms for any investment contract or profit generation implementation. For accounting purposes, tangibility and value are considerations.

Digital Currency has economic, technical, utilitarian, or financial value through an underlying economy, technology, feature, function, or activity. Digital Certificate of Value and Digital Equity represent underlying supporting assets or are manifestations of an asset without underlying assets. All in addition to possessing inherent value as Stores of Value.

THE STRUCTURE OF THE DIGITAL ECONOMY

The exchange traded Digital Economy is separated into four asset classes: Digital Commodities, Digital Currencies, Digital Certificates of Value, Digital Equities.

Digital Commodity

Definition (defined here): A "Digital Commodity" is a consensus of trust and confidence; its value exists on its own without an underlying economy. A Digital Commodity can be perceived to be scarce, in limited supply, difficult or expensive to divide, extract, use, or transfer. A Digital Commodity is fungible. Fungible assets are not unique to one another, are the same in character, and are interchangeable.

Examples: Gold, Silver, Pork Bellies, Natural Gas, Oil, Bitcoin. One bar of 24-carat gold is the same as another bar of 24-carat gold. One Bitcoin is the same as another Bitcoin in its character.

Defining the Digital Economy
Lori Jo Underhill

Digital Currency

Definition (defined here): A "Digital Currency" requires a consensus of trust, confidence; is a unit of account, divisible, stable, accepted; measured against other assets or currencies of value; possibly regulated by authority or governance framework; and supported by an underlying technology, utility, activity, or economy. It may have value or utility within its underlying micro economy; and may, or may not, have any value outside of the underlying economy. Currencies are generated or destroyed as needed for utilization by the underlying economy by the authority or governance framework. Currencies are fungible. Fungible assets are not unique to one another, are the same in character, and are interchangeable.

Examples: EUR, USD, CHF, JPY, EOS, ETH, XRP. One Euro is the same as another Euro, and one Ether is the same as another Ether in its character.

Digital Certificate of Value

Definition (defined here): A "Digital Certificate of Value" has inherent value as a representation of a certificate that can be presented to the underlying asset custodian in exchange for the actual underlying asset (tangible, intangible, Digital Commodity or currency), in proportionate value as identified by the governance framework of the Digital Asset. Digital Certificates of Value are generally fungible. Fungible assets are not unique to one another, are the same in character, and are interchangeable.

Examples: The United States Dollar before the gold standard was abolished. The Gemini Dollar or Tether backed by the United States Dollar. The Carat backed by Diamonds. Any Digital Asset that has an underlying asset held in custody and can be redeemed for the underlying asset. Divisibility is a consideration in the analysis. One Gemini Dollar is the same as another Gemini Dollar in its character. These Digital Assets are sometimes referred to as "Stable Coins."

Defining the Digital Economy
Lori Jo Underhill

Digital Equity

Definition (defined here): A "Digital Equity" is a representation of an ownership interest; whole or fractional, tangible or intangible. A market may or may not exist in consensus for the value of the underlying property. A Digital Equity is difficult or impossible to divide. A Digital Equity is non-fungible. A non-fungible asset is unique in its characteristic as a representation of another asset or item, or the manifestation of one unique and serialized intangible or tangible asset or item. Digital Equities are unique to one another, distinct in character, and not interchangeable.

Examples: Unique Shares of an Entity, Ownership in Real Property, Cryptokitties, Bonds, Shares in Financial Products, Unique Artwork, Jewelry, or Couture Fashion. Any asset that is indivisible, serialized, or unique.

Blockchain, Distributed, Decentralized, Public, Private, and Hyper Ledger Technologies can utilize items that have no economic value; yet are useful and functional, and are not a part of the Digital Economy.

Digital Unit

Definition (defined here): A "Digital Unit" is a piece of software that is functional and useful, is not an asset, has no inherent financial value, external economic value, and does not represent an asset or a store of value that has financial value. It could be fungible or non-fungible depending on its use case. The supply of the software could be finite or infinite depending on its use case. The software can be a manifestation of something, or represent something underlying that may, or may not, have utilitarian or economic value; however, the unit itself has no financial value.

Examples: A Vote, Identity, Digital Container, Measurement, Store of Information, or Store of Data.

Defining the Digital Economy
Lori Jo Underhill

Best Practices Opinion: The evolution and integration of this construct would suggest, as best practice, for entities to issue both Digital Currencies and Digital Equities in the future; thereby, delineating one function as a fungible currency operable within its underlying Digital Economy, and one function as a non-fungible equity share in the entity. Therefore, each would be regulated by the appropriate authority.

CHAPTER 9

THE NEW AGE OF MONEY

It is the dawn of a New Age of Finance.

These technologies challenge the very basic understanding and definition of what the world has understood about economies and money since it has evolved into a Representative Construct.[51] There is fear, uncertainty, and doubt (FUD) because of the lack of information, understanding, and context.

Satoshi Nakamoto's work changed the world's transaction landscape forever. The vision and implementation were not fully understood at the beginning. Satoshi Nakamoto's vision as stated in his Whitepaper[52]:

> *"What is needed is an electronic payment system based on cryptographic proof instead of trust, allowing any two willing parties to transact directly with each other without the need for a trusted third party. Transactions that are computationally impractical to reverse would protect sellers from fraud, and routine escrow mechanisms could easily be implemented to protect buyers. In this paper, we propose a solution to the double-spending problem using a peer-to-peer distributed timestamp server to generate computational proof of the chronological order of transactions. The system is secure as long as honest nodes collectively control more CPU power than any cooperating group of attacker nodes."*

---

[51] "Representative Construct" A system of asset representation that utilizes a substitute for an underlying asset or economy as money.

[52] Nakamoto, S.: "Bitcoin: A Peer-to-Peer Electronic Cash System." https://bitcoin.org/bitcoin.pdf/ (October 31, 2008, accessed September 22, 2018)

Defining the Digital Economy
Lori Jo Underhill

"Crypto-currencies" have caused discussion, disruption, fascination, elation, confusion, anger, frustration, dismay, fear, and pushback from interested parties. The process of Digital Asset integration has started. Now is the time for contextual understanding, adoption, and acceptance. This writing is just a glimpse into the possibilities for utilizing the DASH construct to clarify definition in this space.

Nakamoto stated: "What is needed is an electronic payment system…" The vision is now realized.

What was needed and now available, through the DASH construct discussed in this writing, is a coherent framework of fundamental contextual definitions for instruments operating in the Digital Economy. This framework allows effective integration and adoption for Digital Assets as financial instruments, rather than the disruption or destruction of the existing ecosystem.

Economies are a consensus of agreement. Applying and utilizing a coherent effective construct will streamline and swiftly usher-in the utilization of these powerful technologies collectively; offering innovation and systems likely to transform world finance.

It is happening now; these technologies are the future of money and are touching all economic sectors of the world economy.

It is a pivotal time in the history of the world.

While not all the current market participants will stand the test of time, each technology solution, Digital Asset, instrument, or utilitarian digital ledger technology innovation in the Digital Economy offers a contribution to overall financial and technological evolution.

The United States could be the model for the future of finance, by leading, rather than following the rest of the world in welcoming these new instruments into its economy.

The time is now to get in front of this and get it right.

We may not have the ability to measure this transformation for quite some time. In the meantime, embracing solutions that the technologies offer, participating in the journey of evolution through consensus of definition, educated decision, and adoption will usher-in transformation. Understanding Digital Assets through objective context, information, and knowledge will pave the path to adoption. The frictionless possibilities are available right now in the Digital Economy. The apparent opportunities are boundless. It is not yet known or understood what the future landscape will look like.

HODL[53]. Welcome to the Next Gen of Money.

---

[53] "HODL" A term used in Digital "Crypto-currency" circles that means "Hold on For Dear Life" It originated in a December 2013 post on the Bitcoin Forum message board by an apparently inebriated user who posted with a typo in the subject, "I AM HODLING." rather than HOLDING https://en.wikipedia.org/wiki/Hodl/ (accessed September 22, 2018)

Defining the Digital Economy
Lori Jo Underhill

Lori Jo Underhill B.S., J.D. is a Digital Economy Analyst, "Digital Economist".

Bachelor of Science in Business Administration from Arizona State University in Tempe, Arizona, USA, and Juris Doctor from Southwestern Law School in Los Angeles, California, USA. Lori currently works as an Executive Consultant with over 30 years of experience in hardware and software technology and media.
https://www.linkedin.com/in/lori-jo-underhill/

For more information visit LJU and Associates to learn more about the DASH – Digital Asset Sector Hierarchy™ methodologies and related content.
https://www.ljuassociates.com

Visit www.CoinSector.io for a visualization of the DASH – Digital Asset Sector Hierarchy™ construct.
https://www.coinsector.io

Made in United States
Orlando, FL
14 July 2024